Manners Help THE WORLD GO ROUND!

ZABED MOHAMMAD, PHD.
EDUCATOR & RESEARCHER
CANADA

EDITED BY
ROBERT HART

Copyright © 2023 by Zabed Mohammad,
All rights reserved
CANADA.

Library of Congress Cataloging-in-Publication Data
ISBN: 978-1-998923-19-9

Publisher
Kids Edu Care Inc.
Children's Dedicated Learning Series
Website: www.kidseducare.ca
Illustration Copyright © 2023 by
Kids Edu Care Inc.
Canada

Illustration & Design
Bee Digital

beedigital.asia

info@beedigital.asia

THERE IS AN EXPRESSION THAT GOES, "GOOD MANNERS ARE THE GREASE THAT HELPS THE WHEELS OF HUMAN SOCIETY RUN SMOOTHLY," AND IT IS TRUE! WITHOUT MANNERS, MANY THINGS IN OUR DAY-TO-DAY LIVES WOULD BE MORE DIFFICULT.

FOR EXAMPLE, SIMPLY SAYING “HELLO” TO PEOPLE WHEN WE MEET THEM, AND SAYING “GOODBYE” TO THEM WHEN WE PART, ARE IMPORTANT BECAUSE IT SHOWS THAT WE RESPECT THEM.

SAYING “PLEASE” AND “THANK YOU” IS ALSO IMPORTANT, BECAUSE IT SHOWS GRATITUDE FOR THE THINGS OTHERS DO FOR YOU.

SMILING AND INTRODUCING OTHERS TO YOUR FRIENDS OR FAMILY WHEN THEY COME TO TALK OR VISIT ALSO SHOWS GOOD MANNERS,

BECAUSE IT SHOWS THEY ARE WELCOME IN YOUR GROUP!

COVERING YOUR NOSE AND MOUTH WHEN YOU SNEEZE OR COUGH IS VERY GOOD MANNERS, BECAUSE GERMS ARE GROSS!

WHEN SHARING A MEAL WITH PEOPLE,
IF YOU WANT SOMETHING,
IT IS GOOD MANNERS TO ASK
SOMEONE TO PASS IT INSTEAD OF
REACHING ACROSS THE TABLE.

IT IS ALSO IMPORTANT TO KNOCK ON THE DOOR AND WAIT FOR PERMISSION BEFORE ENTERING A ROOM. ESPECIALLY THE

BATHROOM!

RESPONDING WHEN SOMEONE
ASKS HOW YOU ARE ALSO SHOWS
GOOD MANNERS,
AS IS ASKING HOW THEY ARE, TOO.

NOT INTERRUPTING WHEN OTHERS ARE TALKING IS VERY IMPORTANT.

WAIT FOR YOUR TURN,

NO MATTER HOW IMPATIENT YOU FEEL.

ALSO, SAYING
"EXCUSE ME"
WHEN YOU NEED TO INTERRUPT
A CONVERSATION IS A SIGN OF GOOD MANNERS.
SOMETIMES IT'S AN EMERGENCY,
BUT EVEN SO,
IT IS IMPORTANT TO BE POLITE.

IT IS ALSO IMPORTANT TO SAY

"EXCUSE ME"

IF YOU BUMP INTO SOMEONE.
THIS WAY THEY KNOW YOU DIDN'T
DO IT ON PURPOSE.

NOT READING BOOKS OR USING
ELECTRONICS AT THE DINNER TABLE
WITH OTHERS SHOWS THAT YOU HAVE
GOOD MANNERS BECAUSE
IT SHOWS THEM THAT
THEY ARE IMPORTANT TO YOU.

GOOD MANNERS SOMETIMES MEANS JUST SITTING ATTENTIVELY THROUGH PLAYS, MOVIES, OR MUSICAL PERFORMANCES. THIS SHOWS RESPECT, EVEN IF REALLY, YOU'RE VERY BORED.

WASHING YOUR HANDS BEFORE MEALS
NOT ONLY SHOWS GOOD MANNERS,
IT IS EXTREMELY IMPORTANT
FOR GOOD HYGIENE, TOO.

NO ONE WANTS A

"DIRTY BIRDY"

AT THE TABLE!

UNLESS YOU ARE GOOD FRIENDS
WITH SOMEONE,
IT IS IMPORTANT
TO NOT COMMENT ON THEIR
GROOMING OR APPEARANCE.
IT CAN HURT THEIR FEELINGS
UNNECESSARILY, AND THAT IS DEFINITELY

NOT GOOD MANNERS!

HOLDING DOORS OPEN FOR OTHERS
ALSO SHOWS GOOD MANNERS.

NO ONE LIKES TO HAVE A DOOR
CLOSE ON THEM JUST AS THEY ARE
ENTERING
A ROOM OR BUILDING.

JUST LIKE WITH SNEEZING OR COUGHING,
IT IS VERY IMPORTANT TO COVER
YOUR MOUTH
IF YOU HAVE TO BURP.

AND REMEMBER TO SAY

"EXCUSE ME"

AFTERWARD!

OFFERING TO HELP OTHERS
IF THEY MIGHT NEED
IT IS VERY GOOD MANNERS!
PEOPLE WILL BE GRATEFUL
IF YOU HELP THEM WASH THEIR CAR
OR CARRY THEIR GROCERIES.

IT IS VERY IMPORTANT
TO ALWAYS GIVE A GENUINE APOLOGY
IF YOU MAKE A MISTAKE OR
HURT SOMEONE'S FEELINGS BY ACCIDENT.
SOMETIMES, THE OTHER PERSON JUST NEEDS TO HEAR YOU SAY,

"I'M SORRY."

ASKING TO BE EXCUSED
AT THE END OF A MEAL
ALSO SHOWS GOOD MANNERS.
INSTEAD OF JUST GETTING UP TO LEAVE, SAY,

"MAY I PLEASE BE EXCUSED?"

USING GOOD TABLE MANNERS
WHEN EATING SHOULD GO WITHOUT SAYING.
USE YOUR UTENSILS PROPERLY
AND CHEW QUIETLY,
AND WITH YOUR MOUTH CLOSED!

IT IS IMPORTANT TO TRY
TO SHOW A POSITIVE ATTITUDE,
EVEN IF YOU ARE HAVING
A ROTTEN DAY.
THEN YOU WILL BE SOMEONE THAT
PEOPLE ENJOY HAVING AROUND.

SHAKING HANDS WHEN
YOU MEET SOMEONE,
WHETHER A FRIEND OR A STRANGER,
IS A SIGN OF GOOD MANNERS.
A FIRM HANDSHAKE MAKES
A GOOD IMPRESSION
WHEN YOU MEET SOMEONE.

ALWAYS RETURN ITEMS AFTER YOU BORROW THEM. THIS SHOWS RESPECT FOR OTHER PEOPLE'S BELONGINGS, AND ALSO SHOWS THAT YOU ARE A TRUSTWORTHY PERSON!

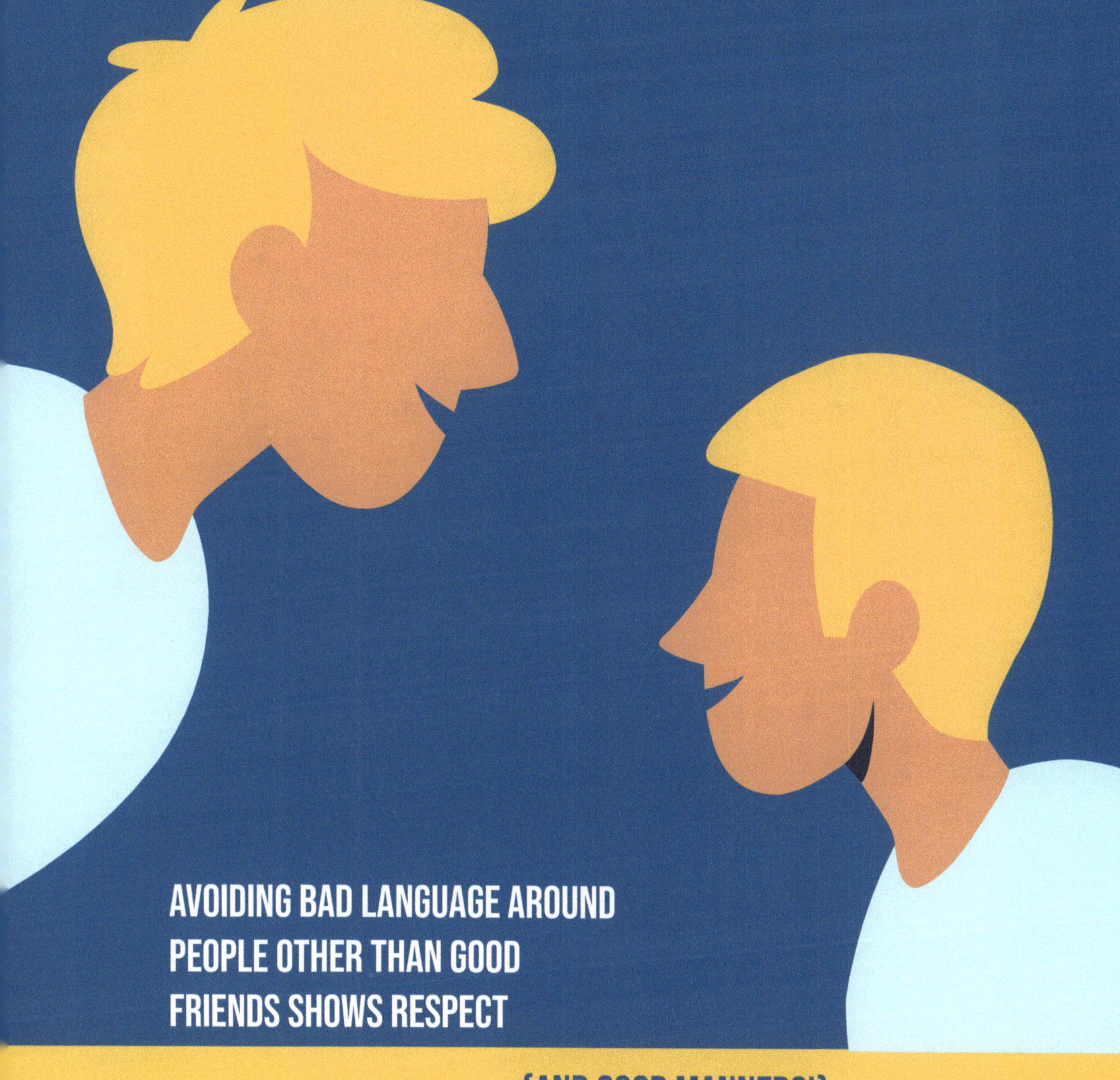

AVOIDING BAD LANGUAGE AROUND
PEOPLE OTHER THAN GOOD
FRIENDS SHOWS RESPECT

(AND GOOD MANNERS!)
FOR THOSE AROUND YOU.
REMEMBER,
THE WORDS YOU USE CAN
REVEAL YOUR CHARACTER.

SHARING IS AN IMPORTANT SIGN OF

GOOD MANNERS,

AND IS A VERY BASIC WAY TO SHOW
CONSIDERATION FOR THE NEEDS
AND FEELINGS OF OTHERS.

GIVING COMPLIMENTS WHEN DESERVED ALSO SHOWS

GOOD MANNERS,

BECAUSE EVERYONE LIKES TO HEAR NICE THINGS ABOUT THEMSELVES!

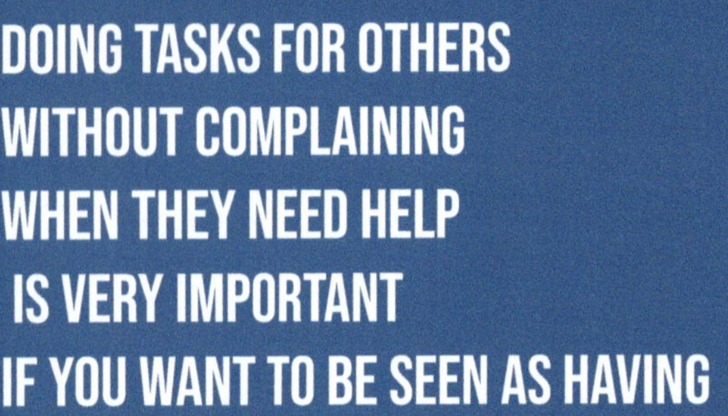

DOING TASKS FOR OTHERS
WITHOUT COMPLAINING
WHEN THEY NEED HELP
IS VERY IMPORTANT
IF YOU WANT TO BE SEEN AS HAVING

GOOD MANNERS.

IF THEY ARE HAVING A
HARD TIME, HELPING THEM
CAN MAKE THEIR DAY BETTER!

WRITING ACTUAL

THANK-YOU

NOTES WHEN YOU RECEIVE GIFTS SHOWS BOTH RESPECT AND APPRECIATION. THINGS LIKE EMAILS OR TEXTS ARE GREAT UNDER NORMAL CIRCUMSTANCES, BUT PEOPLE LIKE A MORE PERSONAL TOUCH AFTER THEY HAVE DONE SOMETHING NICE FOR YOU.

LASTLY,

ALWAYS FOLLOW THE GOLDEN RULE!
TREATING OTHERS H OW YOU WOULD LIKE TO
BE TREATED IS ALWAYS AN
IMPORTANT SIGN OF GOOD MANNERS!
IF YOU REMEMBER THIS RULE,
IT'S ALSO MUCH EASIER TO
FOLLOW ALL THE OTHERS!

Kids Edu Care Canada

Other books you may enjoy

- Kids' First Arabic Words: Alif to Yaa
- Are We Grateful Enough?
- Eid al-Fitr: A Day of Joy for All
- Greetings: What are They Good For?
- I don't care! Wait a moment! We care!
- Who Are We In The World?
- Love For All
- What is Fair?
- I am Searching! Wait a minute! We are searching too!
- We May Look Different
- Work Hard, Dream Big
- I am Curious! Who Created Us?
- Welcoming Ramadan: For Kids
- Universal Brotherhood
- Universal Greetings
- All life Important
- Manners Help the World Go Round
- Attitude Matters

www.ingramcontent.com/pod-product-compliance
Lightning Source LLC
LaVergne TN
LVHW071130160826
845679LV00005B/1240

* 9 7 8 1 9 9 8 9 2 3 1 9 9 *